SHEPHERD'S
V O I C E

Other Books by Bo Sanchez:

Inspirational
How to Live a Life of Miracles
40 Stories of Passion
Don't Worry, Be Happy
How to Turn Thoughts
  into Things
How to Conquer Your Goliaths
Memoirs of a Great Person
How Your Word Can Change
  Your World
My Conspiracy Theory
Five Things You Need to Do
  Before You Die
God Is Bigger Than Your Biggest
  Problem
How to Be a Blessing Magnet
Take Charge, Give All

Personal Finance Series
8 Secrets of the Truly Rich
Simplify and Live
  the Good Life
Simplify and Create Abundance
My Maid Invests in the
  Stock Market
8 Sikreto Para Maging Tunay
  na Mayaman
How to Prosper
The Turtle Always Wins

Kerygma Collection
How to Be Really, Really, Really
Happy (1st Collection)
You Can Make Your life
Beautiful (2nd Collection)
You Have the Power to
  Create Love (3rd Collection)
Fill Your Life with Miracles (4th
Collection)

Healing Series
Your Past Does Not Define
  Your Future
Stop Hidden Addictions
Awaken the Healer in You

Singles & Relationships
How to Find Your
  One True Love
How to Find Your
  One True Love, Book 2
40 Stories of Finding Your
  One True Love
How to Build a Happy Family

Children's Book
Eagles Don't Fly, They Soar!

Bo's Websites:
Read Bo's Blogs at
www.BoSanchez.ph
Watch Bo's Videos
at **www.PreacherInBlueJeans.com**
Get Daily Spiritual Food
at **www.KerygmaFamily.com**
Gain Financial Abundance
at **www.TrulyRichClub.com**
Receive Daily Messages
at **www.GodWhispersClub.com**
Achieve Optimum Health
at **www.HealerInYou.com**
Renew Your Family Life
at **www.FamilyReborn.com**
Learn How to Find Your One True Love
at **www.OneTrueLoveClub.com**

Take Charge, Give All

*7 Steps to Determine Your Destiny
and Create Incredible Success in Your Life*

BO SANCHEZ

#1 National Bestselling Author of *God Is Bigger than Your Biggest Problems*

Take Charge, Give All
7 Steps to Determine Your Destiny
and Create Incredible Success in Your Life

ISBN 978-971-007-058-9

BO SANCHEZ

Philippine Copyright © 2012 by Eugenio R. Sanchez, Jr.
1st Reprinting, February 2013

Address requests for information to:
SHEPHERD'S VOICE PUBLICATIONS, INC.
#60 Chicago St., Cubao, Quezon City, Philippines 1109
P.O. Box 1331 Quezon City Central Post Office
1153 Quezon City
Tel. No. (632) 725-9999, 725-1115, 725-1190, 411-7874
Fax. No. (632) 727-5615, 726-9918
E-mail: sales@shepherdsvoice.com.ph

Cover Design and Layout by Rey de Guzman

Table of Contents

Introduction

Feel Stuck? Here's the Solution...

Everywhere I go, I see deep frustration around me.

People feel "stuck."

They don't know what to do.

They're imprisoned by their present problems.

They want to go forward with their dreams but they're lost.

They want to succeed in life, but nothing is happening.

No matter how much they pray.

No matter how much they read the Bible.

And they ask me, "Bo, what should I do? How can I get unstuck and finally become successful in life?"

If I know that someone's heart is already in the right place, then I give them the *only* solution I know to get unstuck.

I tell them…

"Take charge. Give all."

1. Take Charge

I'm writing this in Room 1517.

At the Waldorf Astoria Hotel in New York City.

Staying in this luxurious hotel with me are regular guys like myself and President Barack Obama, plus a few other heads of states.

I'm not kidding!

I'm a delegate to the 64th General Assembly of the United Nations. Don't ask me to explain why I became one. It's a long story.

But I'm sharing with you this bit of information to tell you that I saw the big guys at close range.

Yesterday, it was too close. I was in the lobby, typing on my laptop, not realizing that I was sitting right beside an incoming train of presidents. I also saw their big bodyguards in sleek black suits, wearing the typical earpiece in one ear. I felt like I was in a movie. I was waiting for James Bond to come in.

That was when one bodyguard the size of Goliath approached me and asked whether I was a dignitary. I wanted to tell them that I was a son of God, but thankfully, I didn't. Or I would still be in some undisclosed prison, interrogated for being a religious nutcase with a sinister plan to bomb the world. When I said "No," he asked me (very kindly) if I could vacate my seat for some royalty in flowing white robes and a turban.

At close range, I realized that world leaders are ordinary human beings.

I noticed that these modern-day kings had two arms, two legs and one head. I was disappointed that none of them had an extra arm, an extra head or the powers of Professor X.

Over the years, I've also worked with CEOs of companies and even founders of churches with millions of members. It's amazing how human everyone is.

But I believe what sets them apart is their ability to lead *themselves.*

Sure, they know how to lead others.

But before they can lead others, they need to lead themselves.

You can't lead your nation, your company, your department, your business, your group or even your kids if you can't lead yourself.

Second solution…

2. Give All

Champions take charge.

And they give their all.

Both go together.

From my experience, it's very difficult to take charge and not give your all. (You probably can, but there'll be something wrong about it.)

Look at the champions of the world...

Why is Manny Pacquiao the best pound-for-pound boxing champion in the world?

You and I only see what Manny does in the ring.

We don't see what he does *outside* the ring.

For example, I can do 10 sit-ups comfortably.

One day, to impress my wife, I tried doing 30 sit-ups. I only reached 25. After that, she had to carry me to bed.

Do you know how many sit-ups Manny Pacquiao does in a day? 100? 200? 500? 1,000?

Nope.

He does 3,000. Every single day.

No wonder he's a champ.

No wonder his abs are like steel.

When he's training before a fight, he starts at 5:30 a.m. and ends at 4:00 p.m. from Monday to Saturday.

That's more than 10 hours of rigorous, grueling, hardcore, violent training. Every day!

In fact, Coach Freddie Roach says that Manny has one weakness: "Manny has a tendency to over-train. I have to stop him." That's dedication.

Why is Manny a champion in boxing?

Because he knows the secret of big returns: He gives his all.

The Guy Who Couldn't Miss a Shot

Larry Bird was one of the best basketball players in the history of the game.

He was known for his shooting magic.

But it was no magic. It was practice.

After every team practice, he'd be the last player to leave the gym. While everyone else was taking a shower in the lockers, Larry would turn off the lights in the court and practice shooting in semi-darkness. Many times, he'd practice three-point shots while closing his eyes. He'd do that every day.

One day, Larry Bird was making a commercial. The director instructed him to miss a shot. That was what the scene required. But because of his muscle memory, Larry had to take 10 shots before he missed one!

Why was Larry a champion in basketball?

Because he knew the secret of big returns: He gave his all.

Diabetes Couldn't Stop Him from Dancing

Gary Valenciano is "Mr. Pure Energy."

He's the only entertainer that has won the Awit Awards for Best Male Performer 11 times!

Yet this man has had Type 1 juvenile diabetes since he was 14 years old. So far, he's had 90,000 insulin injections in his body. Yet his sickness has not stopped him from giving his all every single time he's on stage.

Why is Gary a champion in entertainment?

Because he knows the secret of big returns: He gives his all.

Broken Bones Come with His Job

Jackie Chan is one of the most successful action movie stars in the world today. He's big both in Hong Kong and Hollywood.

Jackie appears twice in the *Guinness Book of World Records*.

First, he holds the record for "most stunts by a

living actor." In fact, no insurance company is willing to insure him.

Because of his movies, he has fractured his skull, dislocated his pelvis, broken his fingers, toes, nose, both cheekbones, hips, sternum, neck, ankle and ribs many times.

Second, he holds the world record for the most number of takes for a single shot in a movie. To make one scene perfect, Jackie had to shoot 2,900 retakes of one scene!

Talk about dedication to his craft.

That's Jackie Chan.

Why is Jackie a champion in action movies?

Because he knows the secret of big returns: He gives his all.

The Most Admired Person in the 20th Century

Blessed Mother Teresa was called a living saint.

According to Gallup polls, survey after survey shows that even while she was still alive, Mother Teresa was already the single most admired person in the 20th century.

She served the poorest of the poor for 45 years.

When she passed away, she left the world with 4,000 nuns that ran 610 centers in 123 countries.

Why has she inspired millions of people?

Because she gave her all.

The Bible says, "Whoever sows sparingly will also reap sparingly, and whoever sows generously will also reap generously" (2 Corinthians 9:6, NLT).

It's really the Law of the Harvest.

What you plant, you harvest.

If you plant small, you harvest small.

If you plant big, you harvest big.

And if you plant all, you harvest all!

Seven Critical Battlegrounds of Life

There's a war in your life.

In the next few pages, I invite you to take charge and give your all in these seven crucial areas:

1. Focus
2. Identity
3. Emotions
4. Values
5. Time
6. Talent
7. Treasure

Are you ready to determine your destiny and create incredible success?

Turn the page…

May your dreams come true,

Bo Sanchez

P.S. Get a mountain of spiritual nourishment for FREE at www.KerygmaFamily.com now! And join our borderless, international, non-physical community!

P.S.2. **Get a unique, inspiring, powerful, personalized message from God each day.** Absolutely FREE! It'll blow you away. Sign up at www.GodWhispersClub.com now!

Take Charge of Your Focus

*Because Your Focus
Becomes Your Reality*

Experience is not what happens to you. Experience is what you do to what happens to you.

Chapter 1

Define Your Experience

Imagine you went to Baguio with your friends.

Everyone had a great time.

From the start, you were already mesmerized by Kennon Road's zigzags. And for the next two days, you rode horses in Wright Park, went boating in Burnham Park, picnicked in Camp John Hay, and climbed the steps to the Lourdes Grotto.

While waiting for the bus home, one of your friends bought a bag of peanuts from the sidewalk.

Munching them all the way down Marcos Highway, she discovered they were rancid.

She spat them out in disgust.

The next day, you meet up with your friends and recount the fabulous time you had in Baguio. Everyone is speaking happily except one person.

You ask her, "What's wrong? Didn't you like Baguio?"

She shakes her head.

"Why?"

She frowns. "The peanuts were rancid."

Your jaw drops. "What?"

"I hate Baguio. Aren't there any government regulations controlling what they sell on their streets? I was deceived by that street vendor. Baguio people are really cheats and liars. And its government is totally inept!"

Insane?

I believe we do exactly the same thing with life.

Beauty or Peanuts

Life is like Baguio.

It's filled with beautiful hills and zigzag roads, horse trails and boat rides, pine trees and fresh air — but we tend to focus on the rancid bag of problems and be disgusted with life in general.

Always remember: *Experience is not what happens to you. Experience is what you do to what happens to you.*

Your life is not about events. Your life is about the interpretation that you give to those events. And you have the power to place whatever interpretation you want to an event.

How?

By the power of focus.

Chapter 2

Choose from a Billion Stimuli

If you've heard me say this before, be patient.

But it's such a great example, I have to share it with you.

One day, while giving a seminar, I announced, "Let's do an experiment."

I asked my audience to locate red things around the room.

"Shirts, books, flags, shoes, bracelets, nail polish, lipstick, and any person bleeding to death…"

After they explored the room for a few seconds, I told them to shut their eyes.

"With your imagination, I want you to recreate a picture of the room in your mind. Do you see it?"

"Yes," they intoned like obedient yogis, still with their eyes closed.

"Good. Now tell me all the objects in the room that you recall are color... *blue!*"

People broke out laughing and had a difficult time naming them.

When I asked them to open their eyes and start looking around, some were surprised that the chairs they were sitting on were blue, that the walls around them were blue, that their depressed seatmate was blue (sorry for this corny joke).

Why did this happen?

Because of the power of *focus.*

When you're focused on one object — like the color red — it will be very difficult to see anything else — like the color blue.

Let me tell you how this works.

Why We Don't See Blue

Right this minute, there's a ton of stimuli that's bombarding your five senses.

There are colors, smells, lights, people, different movements — a tidal wave of information that your brain has to process.

Do you know what keeps you sane amidst the avalanche of data?

Your brain has the ability to focus.

It has a *selective mechanism* where it chooses what it will accept and reject. In fact, scientists believe that you only perceive *one in a billion stimuli!*

Here's my key to success: ***Learn to control your focus.***

Which one in a billion of data will you focus on?

Determine your focus and you'll determine your reality.

Here's one powerful way of doing this…

Do you wish to enter the Promised Land? You have to first of all conquer the giants in your mind.

Chapter 3

Focus on the Dream

Let me tell you the story of the 12 spies in the Bible. Moses sends 12 men to survey Canaan, the Promised Land.

I imagine Moses as Tommy Lee Jones, firing off instructions in machine-gun fashion, "Listen up, men. I want you to scout the land in and out. Check out its food supply. Bring home specimens. Take soil samples. Get a water analysis. And the air pollution index. Shoot photos. Give me videos. Go, go, go!"

So these guys march off and, after 40 days, return with the goods.

Two guys — Joshua and Caleb — are all revved up and ready to conquer the land. Like giggly teenagers before their prom night, they're excited and can't stand still. They tell Moses, "Let's go, go, go! Let's get this land! Tomorrow! Today! Now! *Yesterday!*"

But the other 10 guys are the opposite picture. They come home with drooped shoulders and bent backs, singing the blues. Here's what they say…

"We can't attack those people; they are stronger than we are." And they spread among the Israelites a bad report about the land they had explored. They said, "The land we explored devours those living in it. All the people we saw there are of great size.... We seemed like grasshoppers in our own eyes, and we looked the same to them."[1]

Grasshopper Mentality

You know how stories go around.

One of the spies say, "I saw huge men!"

"Huge? How huge?"

"One man's leg is bigger than your mother's waist!"

"Wow."

And the message gets passed along...

"Hey, I heard the men in that land are so gigantic, each man's leg is bigger than my mother and your mother and your neighbor's mother *combined*."

"My gosh..."

And the message gets passed along further...

"Have you heard? The men in that land will *eat* all our mothers like they're munching grasshoppers!"

And the message gets passed along further and further...

---

[1] *Numbers 13:31-33, NIV*

"We're doomed! We're grasshoppers! Let's go back to Egypt!"

Negative Response

According to the Bible, the Israelites grumbled, complained, and picketed in front of Moses, demanding that they go back to Egypt.[2]

Let me refresh your memory on some recent Steven Spielberg-type events that happened prior to this moment.

- Moses had just parted the Red Sea.
- Pharaoh's chariots, the greatest army on the planet, sank in the Red Sea.
- Manna fell from the sky like it was rain.
- Quails became as easily accessible as chicken nuggets.
- A rock turned into a giant water cooler.

And yet it seemed no one remembered these miracles at all.

Why?

Because their brain's selective mechanism made a decision to focus on the giants.

---

[2] *Numbers 14:1f*

Don't Focus on the Giants

The Israelite spies did their "scouting" for 40 days — and because they focused on the giants in the land — they had to suffer for 40 *years* with imaginary giants in their minds.

What should have been a few months' travel became 40 years in the desert. (Does this sound like life to you? It sure does to me.)

When the Israelites finally crossed into the Promised Land, there were only two men from the former generation who were able to enter it — Joshua and Caleb — the two spies who focused on the milk and honey, not on the giants of the land.

Friend, do you wish to enter the Promised Land?

You have to first of all conquer the giants in your mind.

Problems with your inadequacy. Problems with money. Problems with your parents. Problems with your children. Problems with your work.

Sure, they're giants.

If you focus on them, you'll forget the biggest Giant of them all. "Because greater is He that is in you than he that is in the world!"[3]

Take charge of your focus!

---

[3] *1 John 4:4 (ASV)*

Action Steps

Take Charge of Your Focus

1. On what have you been regularly focusing your thoughts? On what you want to do or on your fears? On the giants outside or on the Giant inside you?

2. Think of one area in your life where you should change your focus, from that which causes you misery to thoughts that bring you joy. In what way should you change what your mind dwells on?

3. What kind of "faith" thoughts will you think about?

4. Make a commitment for the next seven days to wake up and ask yourself these powerful questions:
   a) What am I very grateful for in my life right now?
   b) What am I committed to do in my life right now?
   c) Who do I love? And who loves me?

Take Charge of Your Identity

It Will Define Your Level of Success

*Why not **doubt** all the labels you and others have given yourself in the past and really ask if they're true or not?*

Chapter 4

Create an Identity Crisis

Menopause.

I have no idea what menopause is like.

Because I haven't had it (thank God) and I don't intend to have it.

But from what I have read, menopause is an identity crisis. And that's something *I like.*

Before I explain that statement, let me get back to the mystery of menopause.

For women, it's a very physical thing, caused by the lack of a hormone called estrogen. But it's also highly psychological...

Because suddenly, the menopausal woman realizes the number of her white hairs is increasing.

And her cellulite deposits compound daily.

And she looks at her face in the mirror and she almost says, "Hi, Mom!"

And she wonders where her wrinkles came from. The age spots. The leathery skin. The soggy cheeks. The drooping breasts. The baggy neck.

But do you know that there's such a thing as andropause *male* menopause?

No missing hormones here.

It's purely psychological.

When men reach a certain age, they realize that some of their dreams won't be accomplished. Their ambitions for a higher pay, a bigger house, a faster car have escaped them — and there's no more time to pursue them. It slowly dawns on them that some of their dreams are doomed.

And then they ask those ultimate questions in life.

What is life all about?

Where am I going?

Who am I?

Why was I born in this world?

What is the purpose of my life?

Identity Crisis

That's a full-blown identity crisis — and I like that because it causes us to ask those ultimate questions.

You also ask these questions when your doctor tells you that you have cancer and have only six months to live.

You ask these questions when your boss tells you, "Our company is folding up," and suddenly, you're on the street without a job.

You ask these questions when your single daughter tells you, "I'm pregnant," and you wonder what you did wrong.

Don't Wait for One; Create an Identity Crisis!

During moments like these, many people redefine themselves. They rearrange the hierarchy of their values. They realize that the most important things in their lives are not wealth, power, fame, recognition or the admiration of people.

From an identity of "businessman" or "computer programmer" or "yuppie" or "housewife" or "teacher" or even "religious leader" — all those labels fall into third or fourth or fifth place. You grope and struggle for a primary label.

But here's my question: Why wait for a catastrophe? Why wait for menopause? Why wait for cancer to hit you? Why wait for retrenchment?

Why not *manufacture* an identity crisis now?

Why not ask those ultimate questions now?

Why not *doubt* all the labels you and others have given yourself in the past — and really ask if they're true or not?

Even if the identity is totally false, if that's what you perceive yourself to be, it'll be powerful in shaping your life.

Chapter 5

The Power of Perceived Identity

I'm not talking about the power of your identity.

I'm talking about the power of your *perceived* identity.

Meaning, even if the identity is totally false, if that's what you perceive yourself to be, it'll be powerful in shaping your life.

Let me tell you an old story.

One day, a boy was walking up a cliff. Noticing some broken branches between the huge rocks, he went to investigate. His eyes widened when he saw a nest with an egg in it! He looked around, assured himself that it was safe, and grabbed the egg.

The boy took it home and placed it with the other eggs in his chicken house.

A few days later, the egg hatched with the other chicken eggs.

A chick of a different color and size broke through the shell.

But he didn't know he was different. He was just happy that he had little brothers and sisters around him — and a mother that took care of him.

This different chick grew up, pecked on the ground, and made chicken sounds like his siblings — and life went on smoothly.

But one day, a huge bird flew a thousand feet above them, barely seen in the sunlight. All the chickens ran for cover, and the different chick ducked as well.

"Mommy, what was that?" he asked.

"That's an eagle," the mother answered in a quivering voice, "a very strong, swift bird. We can fly only 20 feet up, but an eagle can fly 20,000 feet above us. It can even sleep in a storm. Its eyesight is so sharp, it can spot chickens like you from a thousand feet up in the air. It's the king of the sky."

"Wow. Do they live in chicken houses like ours?"

The mother shook her head. "No. They build their nests in high cliffs amidst the jagged rocks."

And he never realized that, at one time, he was an egg in one such cliff.

He was really an eagle and could fly 20,000 feet in the air.

But because he *perceived* himself as a chicken, he continued to peck on the ground and make chicken sounds for the rest of his life.

God sees stuff that we know nothing about because He put it there from the very beginning. He knows us more than we know ourselves.

Chapter 6

See Yourself As God Sees You

Let me now tell you a story of another chick who realized he was really an eagle — and soared to great heights.

One day, tiny Israel was being attacked and harassed and plundered by the Midianites. The poor Israelites were afraid and went into hiding, making their homes in caves and mountains.

But after seven years of foreign domination, God finally finds a man to lead them to freedom. But it was a rather odd introduction…

The Bible says a man named Gideon was threshing wheat in a winepress — doing it secretly. Why? Like everyone else, he was *hiding* from the Midianites.

And then an angel came and appeared to him saying, "The Lord is with you, brave and mighty man!" (In Tagalog, the angel probably said, "Macho *ka!*")

I'm sure Gideon turned around and looked behind him… and finding no one, he asked the angel, "Uh… Mr. Angel, who are you talking to?"

The angel smiles and points in his direction.

"Me? You… you're talking to me?"

"Uh-huh…"

"Gee, Mr. Angel, thanks for the visit, but I think you've got the wrong address. I mean, someone must have given you wrong directions or something. I'm sure you've got the wrong house! And I'm almost positive you've got the wrong town. I mean (and you can find this in the Bible), my clan is the poorest in the tribe of Mannaseh. In terms of social brackets, we're wedged between class D and E. And not only that, I'm the least, puniest, the most unimportant guy in my family. I'm nothing! I'm dirt! I'm a speck of dust! I'm spit! And I'm here hiding from the Midianites!"

But the angel doesn't even listen to his speech. Instead, he tells him, "Surely I will be with you, and you shall smite the Midianites as one man!" [1]

Here's the key: Gideon started believing in what God told him.

In other words, he began to doubt his past perception of his identity — that he was a coward and a nobody.

---

[1] *Judges 6:1-16*

Instead, Gideon started believing in a new label given by the angel — "brave and mighty man!"

And true enough, years later, with only 300 men, he defeated an army of thousands! Under his hand, the Midianites received their defeat — and the Isrealites were set free.

The Manufacturer Is Always Right

God sees in us what we can't see in ourselves.

He sees stuff that we know nothing about — because He put it there from the very beginning. *He knows us more than we know ourselves.*

I believe that if we get a glimpse of what He sees in us, it will revolutionize our lives.

When all we see is our ugliness — God tells us that we're more beautiful than all the universe.

When all we see is our sinfulness — God tells us that we are holy in the depths of our being.

When all we see are our weaknesses — God says that we are strong beyond our wildest imagination.

Why? Because the Manufacturer made us using the template of His Son Jesus.

We always talk about original sin.

But hand in hand with that doctrine is *original innocence.*

Original beauty.

Original holiness!

Before sin warped our lives, we were made *like* God.

That means in the depths of who we are, we were made kind and loving and good and holy and beautiful!

And each day, if we can only hear God telling us how loving, how gorgeous, how courageous, how faithful, how disciplined, how powerful, how glorious, how passionate, how holy, how beautiful we are — our lives will change!

Chapter 7

You Become the Labels You Give Yourself

Do you want to have the blue eyes of Brad Pitt?

Without the use of colored contact lenses?

Medically, it's *impossible* to change your eye color.

But I've discovered a way to do it.

Let me tell you how.

Dr. Bernie Siegel was a famous surgeon when he was attracted to the world of psychology. And one of the things that fascinated him were multiple personality disorders.

People with multiple personality disorders shift from one personality to another in a blink of an eye. Dr. Siegel had studied patients who had more than 100 personalities!

Let me give you an example of this disorder.

Let's say the patient is exhibiting the personality of a 55-year-old businessman.

And then — wham! — he acts like a 28-year-old housewife.

And two minutes later — wham! — he acts like a three-year-old toddler.

Here's the big discovery. Dr. Siegel noticed biochemical changes in the patient's body when his personality changed.

Let me make this graphic for you. Imagine the 55-year-old businessman has hypertension. (As my friend says, *"Mataas ang* high blood *niya.")*

And then the patient shifts to another personality — that of a 28-year-old housewife.

All of a sudden, his blood pressure becomes normal.

But his sugar level rises and he becomes borderline diabetic.

And then the patient shifts to another personality — that of a three-year-old toddler.

And like magic, his sugar level becomes normal.

Why? That's the power of perceived identity.

And would you believe, right before Dr. Siegel's eyes, he saw lesions disappear on the skin of the patient during his shifts of personality. He even documents one patient who changed eye color during shifts of personality.

So, if you want to have blue eyes, try to develop a multiple personality disorder, and just maybe…

But here's my point: Do you now see the power of perceived identity? It affects you physically, so imagine how much more easily it'll affect your behavior!

Labels Are Powerful

One day, a teacher gave an IQ test to her students. And like any other class, some kids were bright and some were not so bright. Some were even failing.

Days later, this teacher went to her desk and saw a piece of paper listing the names of her pupils and corresponding numbers. She said, "The IQ results are here."

But her eyes almost bulged from their sockets when she realized her kids got scores nearing genius level — including those who were failing!

In her next class, she excitedly told them, "You're intelligent!" The kids were shocked, especially those categorized as not so bright. She told them of their excellent IQ scores. And each day, she related to them as excellent students.

And the kids responded. By the end of the year, their grades went up and they performed very well in school.

Around that same time, she showed the IQ test results that changed the lives of her students to a fellow teacher. The fellow teacher looked at that "historic" piece of paper and raised an eyebrow. "I don't know how to tell you this," she said, "but these aren't IQ test results."

"Of course they are! What do you think they are?" the teacher asked.

"Locker numbers."

And it was true. What she thought were high IQ scores were actually locker numbers for the kids.

But don't you see?

Who you think you are doesn't even have to be true.

It just has to be *perceived* as true — and it will affect your life powerfully.

Here's the truth: **You become the labels you give yourself.**

Chapter 8

How to Change a Label

I experienced this personally.

Let me share my academic life with you.

When you read my books or listen to my preaching, some of you probably imagine me to be a *summa cum laude* or valedictorian in school. (How very humble of me to think so, huh?)

Friends, you can't be farther from the truth.

By Grade 2, I was already failing. I got 72 in math. In panic, Mom got a private tutor for me, and thankfully, my grades went up after a year of great struggle.

I got 75.

Not because I learned to do math, but because the private tutor that mom got and paid for was also my math teacher in school.

Here was the sublime goal of my entire academic life: to *pass*.

My so-so grades continued all the way through high school and college.

I was a permanent C student.

Why? I simply *labeled* myself as average, mediocre, ordinary.

In my eyes, that was who I was.

Changing My Label

But a paradigm shift rocked my world when I was in third year college.

My Catholic community needed a full-time staffer, and I was more than happy to volunteer and say, "I'll serve the Lord and leave my studies!"

And that's just what I did.

But as I did my work, I felt a need to study about God.

So I went to a theological school and spoke to the dean who was also a priest.

"Father, I want to study about God," I said.

He looked at me. "Have you finished college?"

I shook my head, "Not yet."

"Then you can't study here. We just offer masteral programs."

I just kept looking at him and smiled.

"Oh, all right," he blurted out, "you can study here. But I won't be able to give you a diploma. After studying here, get your college diploma and then I'll give you your masters diploma."

"It's OK, Father, I don't care about the diploma. Thank you!"

I went to class with excitement.

I remember my first major exam. In the next class, my professor, who was also the dean, announced to the class, "I'm going to write on the board the names of the top five students with the highest grades in the last exam."

I wasn't even looking.

Someone tapped me on the shoulder and whispered, "Bo, look at the board."

The professor was writing, "Bo Sanchez... Perfect."

I froze.

When the class was over and I was all alone in the room, I walked to the blackboard and stared at my name.

And I almost screamed, *"Don't tell me it was all a lie!"*

My Behavior Changed When My Label Changed

I believed in a lie — the label that I gave myself all those years was "average, mediocre and ordinary." But there was truth staring me in the face, telling me I could be excellent if I put my heart into it!

And so on that day, I changed my label in a snap.

I went through my masteral program with flying colors.

And after two years, I went back to college with a *vengeance*.

How much did my grades change?

Let me tell you a story and you'll get an idea of the great transformation that took place — because of a label change.

One day, I was getting my grades for the semester.

I used to recall how this was such a terrifying ordeal on my part. I'd get ulcers just standing in line. Simply because I didn't know if I'd fail or pass.

But when I went back to college the second time around, I felt totally different.

On that day, my classmate in front of me in the line reminded me of myself years ago: all jittery, with sweaty palms and shaking knees.

"Bo," he asked, "are you nervous, too?"

I didn't want to offend him, so I said, "Yes, I am nervous, too."

But I didn't tell him why I was nervous.

I was nervous about being first honor or second honor.

Yes, my life changed.

Because I *perceived* myself differently.

Here's one of my great realizations: If you want to help someone change his life, don't try changing his behavior. It rarely works.

My mother tried. Believe me. For 20 years, she lectured me to "study, study, study!" Nothing happened.

I repeat. If you want to help someone change, don't try changing his behavior. *Instead, help him change his perceived identity.* And his behavior will change!

Your opinion of yourself will determine the level of your success.

Chapter 9

Believe in God's Opinion of You

Many people have opinions about you.

Your parents, your siblings, your boss, your officemate, your barber, your waiter, your postman — and every person you've met — have opinions about you.

And you really have no control over those opinions. Some are bad, some are good, some are true, and some are garbage.

It's so easy to absorb these opinions and make them your opinion of yourself.

Your opinion of yourself will determine the level of your success.

As a father or mother or husband or wife or child.

As a teacher or nurse or manager or salesman or student.

Even as a Christian.

Imagine if the subconscious label hanging around your neck says, "I'm a lousy mother," or "I'm a dimwitted student," or "I'm an awful manager," or "I'm an unspiritual person."

How miserable you would be!

Change your labels.

But listen: Your Manufacturer has an opinion about you, and it's totally, completely accurate. Because He made every fiber of your being, He knows you more than anyone else. So trust His opinion.

He says…

"If anyone is in Christ, he is a new creation; the old has gone, the new has come!"[4]

Believe.

Action Steps

Take Charge of Your Identity

1. What negative labels do you have that have caused failure in your life? List them down.

2. Does God agree with these labels?

3. Develop an identity crisis right now. Start doubting past definitions of who you are that prevented you from doing what God wants you to do.

4. Do you know that God has given you the incredible power to redefine yourself? Remember: You become the labels you give yourself. So ask Him what new labels you should give yourself.

Take Charge of Your Emotions

*You'll Empower
Your Decisions*

On Judgment Day, God won't ask you, "Did you become emotionally honest?" As corny as it sounds, He will still ask you, "Did you love?"

Chapter 10

How *Not* to Deal with Negative Emotions

I receive a tidal wave of letters from readers every day.

Many of them are about pain.

About fear.

About sadness.

About worry.

About depression.

About rejection.

About low self-worth.

Many letters are from wives whose husbands are adulterers.

Or from parents whose kids are on drugs.

Or from people whose best friends betray them, steal from them, cheat them.

Sometimes I describe my mailbox as "a collection of mutilated hearts that have gone through the blender of human life." Not a pretty picture, believe me.

Here's the truth: We've all gone through that blender.

And because of that, negative emotions are here to stay.

Before I share how we *should* deal with anger, fear, sadness and all the other juicy stuff that come out of the blender, let me share three insane ways of how people commonly deal with negative emotions — and the harm we inflict on ourselves.

1. Don't Avoid Your Emotions

Jorge, a bank supervisor, is 43 years old — and still single.

He complains that he hasn't found the right woman yet.

That women are different now.

That women are overly materialistic.

That women are demanding, self-centered and hysterical.

But the actual truth is that Jorge doesn't want to enter into *any* romantic relationship.

Even if a woman with the heart of Mother Teresa and the body of Catherine Zeta Jones were to flirt with him, he'd still walk the other way.

Why? Twenty years ago, his girlfriend left him for another guy and he was devastated. Crushed. Humiliated. In other words, his heart went through the blender. Since then, he has avoided all relationships so that he won't get hurt again.

Mitch, a 34-year-old woman in the administrative department, is known as a big snob. Her various names in the office restroom include "Mitch the Witch" and "Mitch the Bitch." She has no close friends. But delving deeper, you'll discover that her motto is pretty simple: *I'll reject you first before you reject me.* More than a roaring lion, she is a wounded kitten that's crying out for attention.

Twenty-seven-year-old Judy likes the party life. You'll see her in the thick of the dancing crowd. You'll see her with friends, talking and laughing endlessly. But many know that behind the makeup and toothpaste smile is a profound emptiness. Her boyfriend is a jerk — the fifth in a long line of jerk boyfriends. Her career isn't going anywhere. And deep down, she hates herself. But instead of facing the beautiful ugliness of truth, she drowns her loneliness with the loud music of the bar scene.

Jorge and Mitch and Judy avoid the negative emotions in life — hurt and rejection and loneliness. But here's the problem with avoidance: they don't only avoid the negative emotions, they end up avoiding the positive ones, too — like love, acceptance and true joy.

2. Don't Deny Your Emotions

Virgil has had an ugly conflict with his mother ever since he can remember.

Virgil tries his best to deny his anger. Before he visits her, he mutters beneath his breath a hundred times, "I'm not angry, I'm not angry, I'm not angry…." Upon entering her home, he kisses her on the cheek, and it seems fine for a few minutes. Soon, however, a remark from her about his work, his wife, his kids or his clothes gets his blood boiling again.

Why doesn't this work?

Let me show you why.

Say this aloud:

I'm not thinking of a purple dinosaur.

I'm not thinking of a purple dinosaur.

I'm not thinking of a purple dinosaur.

Repeat this line a thousand more times.

So let me ask you: What are you thinking of?

Let me guess.

A purple dinosaur?

In the same way, denying the existence of your negative emotion won't work either.

When you're angry, you can repeat a thousand times, "I'm not angry!" and your anger will still be there after the thousandth repetition.

When you're sad, when you're lonely, when you're afraid, you can deny these emotions all you want, and they'll still be there staring you in the face.

Denial doesn't work.

3. Don't Be a Slave to Them

Here's the opposite of denial.

"I don't want to be plastic," Roger says, "because I'm no hypocrite. I want to be true to myself — to what I feel. I'm a WYSIWYG person. What you see is what you get."

Sounds wonderful on the surface.

Except that at any given time, Roger is known to blow his top, or fly into a rage, or kick the puppy, or sulk for a year, or badmouth his friends… because that's what he feels at that moment, without any regard for others' feelings.

People like these prioritize *emotional honesty* as the most important thing in the world.

Now, emotional honesty *is* important. It's essential for wholeness, healing and trust in relationships. But it isn't the most important thing in the world.

What is most important? Hands down, it's still love.

On Judgment Day, God won't ask you, "Did you become emotionally honest?" As corny as it sounds, He will still ask, "Did you love?"

Emotional honesty should serve love.

Always.

Chapter 11

Negative Beliefs About Negative Emotions

Why do people deal with emotions in these crazy ways?

Because of wrong beliefs about negative emotions. Here are some of them…

"Families Shouldn't Talk about Painful Topics"

Some of us come from families whose unwritten rule is, "Don't rock the boat." They won't openly talk about their conflicts, or their alcoholic mother, or their unfaithful father, or their sick grandmother, or their financial woes. In other words, they'll talk about the weather, act like a clown, sweep pain under the rug, throw a party every day, declare a cold war for 20 years — just so they won't talk about negative emotions.

"Negative Emotions Aren't Pleasing to God"

Some of us belong to religious groups that don't differentiate negative emotions from negative behavior. They condemn both equally.

Let me give you some of the cruel things Christians say to one another...

- "You're afraid? Worried? Then you're spiritually immature. Where's your trust in God? Proverbs 3:5 says..."
- "You're still angry? That simply means you're still carnal. Operating in the flesh. You're not yet controlled by the Holy Spirit."
- "How can you be sad? You've forgotten that you're a child of God. You've forgotten that you're saved by the Blood and redeemed by the Lamb. If you're sad, that only means you've been listening to the lies of the devil. Ephesians 6 says..."

So when people are angry, or depressed, or fearful, they'll more likely hide it from everyone else — lest they get clobbered with Scripture verses by their well-meaning brethren.

"Saints Don't Have Negative Emotions"

Some people are convinced that holy people don't get afraid, get angry, or get sad. For them, saints only smile and pray the entire day — much like their religious statues on their altar.

People imagine that when holy people are mugged in the street, they speak to the mugger with the warmth of a doting grandmother, "I love you, my son. Wait here. I'll get more money at home for you."

Or when holy people get sick, we imagine them crying out to God, "More pain, Lord. Give me more pain!"

Or when their house burns down or their child dies or they lose their jobs, we imagine them humming a tune, watering their gardens, and waving at everybody that passes by.

Those people don't look like saints to me.

Psychos, yes, but holy people, no.

The holy people I know get afraid, get angry and get sad like everyone else — but just respond to these emotions differently.

"Feelings Mean Weakness"

Action movies usually portray their stars to be square-jawed, muscular, broad-shouldered men who shoot 268 men with their sub-machine gun — all the while chewing gum or smoking a cigar or kissing a girl. It seems that the less emotion they show, the stronger they are.

Baloney.

"Bottom Line, Emotions Are Our Enemies"

Some people view their negative emotions as obstacles to their success. So they fight them, deny them, imprison them, or drive them out. Which is a total waste — because negative emotions can be friends bearing precious gifts to us.

What can these gifts be?

Chapter 12

Treat Your Negative Emotions as Your Friends

For many years, close friends told me I had a problem with denial.

By that, they meant that I denied whatever negative emotions I felt.

Naturally, I denied that I was denying them.

It took a while for me to realize that it was true: I rarely *permitted* myself to feel negative emotions.

Why did I do that?

Because I thought that was what good Christians should do.

"How are you?" people would ask, and the canned answer I taught everyone in my prayer group to say was, "Victorious!" (I even taught people the proper way of saying it — with a raised right arm, a beaming smile, with the emphasis on the second syllable: "vicTORious!")

I taught them to say it in *all* circumstances, quoting the Bible, "Be thankful in all circumstances."[1]

Yep, even if an hour ago, you just got run over by a train that amputated your two legs, your answer should always be, "Victorious! I still have my arms, see?"

OK, that may be an exaggeration, but my philosophy came close.

I believed that any hint of worry meant you didn't trust God.

And any tinge of anger meant you disobeyed the Lord's command to forgive.

And any trace of sadness meant you didn't follow the Bible when it says, "Be joyful always!"[2]

For me, a person who was feeling negative emotions meant that he lacked faith, which meant that he lacked spiritual maturity. So I looked down on them like second-class Christians whom God was tolerating because of His mercy.

Until God hit me on the head.

---

[1] *1 Thessalonians 5:18 (NLT)*
[2] *1 Thessalonians 5:16 (NLT)*

The Bible Tells a Different Story

As I read through the same Bible that I quoted to justify my condemnation of negative emotions, I realized Scripture was *overflowing* with negative emotions!

Elijah wanted to kill himself in utter despair.

Isaiah had self-doubt.

Paul was deeply hurt by his friends — and wrote about it.

Some Psalms spoke about *anger towards God.*

A whole book — Lamentations — is the most depressing book in the world. For five straight chapters, the writer spills his guts out — bitterness, dejection, melancholy, despondency, grief…

And here's the clincher: even Jesus got angry, wept at a friend's death, and became so afraid, He sweat blood.

I was wrong.

Emotions — especially negative ones — have the unique ability to reveal your soul.

Chapter 13

Negative Emotions Are Gifts

Today, I believe the opposite.

I believe that negative emotions are precious gifts from God.

In fact, I believe they do three things…

1. Negative Emotions Are Windows to Your Soul

One day, I felt a nagging emptiness within me.

I found myself… sad.

It wasn't loud or big or dramatic.

It was more like the discomfort one feels when one wears a shoe a half-size too small or big. It was a dull throb surfacing every so often, during brief lulls in my busyness — like when I traveled on a plane, or ate alone, or went home after a huge prayer rally. The feeling was so subtle, so soft, so faint, it was easy to brush it aside.

Paradoxically, I was preaching almost daily, leading dynamic organizations that were impacting the world. I *should* have been feeling fantastic.

But I wasn't.

And I pondered, "What if *this time*, I won't deny what I feel?"

So instead of brushing it aside, I chose to sit down and *feel* my sadness.

I quieted my soul and asked myself, *Where does this sadness come from?*

At first, there was no answer. I couldn't put my finger on it. So I continued feeling the sadness before my God — telling myself it was "OK" to feel sad.

And after a few days, the "window" opened, and I saw my soul: a part of me was saying, "I'm sad because you've lost the purity of your heart."

Yes. There was a time when I did everything from the purest motives.

I preached for God. I preached for love.

But after more than 20 years of preaching, other motives had slowly seeped into my soul unnoticed. Like pride. Self-importance. Seeking special attention. Materialism. Ego-tripping.

As I continued to be patient with my sadness, the window opened even wider, and I could see my soul's wounds in a clearer way. And as I sat and silenced everything else except my sadness before me, I could now hear my soul's words more powerfully. *Return to your first love. Be pure! And I will be happy again!*

I repented.

Each day, I chose to battle for purity of motives.

And like a dark cloud that was blown away by the wind, my sadness vanished.

Remember, you are *not* your emotions.

You are much more than them!

But emotions — especially negative ones — have the unique ability to reveal your soul.

Feel them.

Stay with them.

Search your heart.

Why are you sad? Why are you afraid? Why are you angry?

They will tell you of your deepest desires.

They will share to you your deepest wounds.

And this will make you receive their next gift…

2. Negative Emotions Are a Call to Action

That day, I learned that negative emotions are a "call to action."

First, negative emotions will tell you *where you are.*

Second, negative emotions will guide you to *where you need to go.*

There are people who want to cut short the process. "I don't want to go through this painful emotion. Let me just do what I need to do and get this over with!"

But it doesn't work that way. For how can you know where you should go if you don't know where you are?

But when you know where you are by peeking through the "window" of your negative emotion, you'll be able to chart your course of action.

Sometimes, the action being asked of me is *non-action.* To simply feel the emotion, because by allowing myself to grieve, I'm loving myself.

Sometimes, the action being asked of me is to repent of sin.

Sometimes, the action being asked of me is to tell someone I'm angry, or to ask for forgiveness from someone, or to start a project, or to give up a project, or to persevere in a project.

Usually, this isn't a one-shot deal. You'll have to repeat the action being asked — whatever it is — again and again and again…

Why talk about action?

There are people who permit themselves to feel their negative emotions but stay depressed (or angry or afraid or worried) for 20 years and become totally selfish and rude — not realizing that negative emotions are there to move us to action — *to love God, to love others, and to love oneself.*

And when you do so, you taste the third gift of negative emotions…

3. Negative Emotions Are God's Healing Instruments

If I tell you that God heals us *through* our sadness, our anger, our fears — you'd think I just committed a typographical error.

No. There is no error. What I said is true.

God is a Surgeon, and many times, He heals us through pain.

He takes the scalpel of difficulty, cuts open our life, exposes our diseased parts, and excises the cancerous tissue of our soul.

Sometimes, it's bloody.

Sometimes, you wonder why God is allowing the torture. Sometimes, you actually ask whether He still loves you.

But everything is happening precisely *because* He does. Because He must heal you. Otherwise, He doesn't really care for you.

Chapter 14

How Jesus Dealt with Negative Emotions

Jesus had negative emotions. (Surprise!)
Let's find out how He dealt with them.

(Jesus) took Peter and the two sons of Zebedee along with him, and he began to be sorrowful and troubled. Then he said to them, "My soul is overwhelmed with sorrow to the point of death. Stay here and keep watch with me." Going a little further, he fell with his face to the ground and prayed, **"My Father, if it is possible, may this cup be taken from me. Yet not as I will, but as you will."** *Then he returned to his disciples and found them sleeping. "Could you men not keep watch with me for one hour?" he asked Peter... He went away a second time and prayed,* **"My Father, if it is not possible for this cup to be taken away unless I drink it, may your will**

be done." *When he came back, he again found them sleeping, because their eyes were heavy. So he left them and went away once more and prayed the third time, saying the same thing.*

– Matthew 26:37-40, 42-44 (NIV, emphasis added)

Here are four quick observations from this story.

First, Jesus stayed with the emotion. He didn't deny it, hide it, or escape it. He faced it and He felt it.

Second, He told His friends about it. This is important! He told His Apostles, "My soul is overwhelmed with sorrow…"

Third, He responded to the emotion's call to action: He prayed and surrendered His life to the Father.

Fourth, He kept on repeating the action called for by the emotion — to pray. Don't expect negative emotions to disappear in an instant. It will take repeated action — doing what you need to do — to change your situation.

Let me say it again.

Bless your life and learn from your negative emotions.

Make them your friends, not your enemies.

Action Steps

Take Charge of Your Emotions

1. What negative emotions do you experience often? Identify them.

2. How do you deal with these negative emotions?

3. Do you have wrong beliefs about negative emotions? If so, which ones?

4. What is your negative emotion telling you about yourself? What message or call to action is it offering you?

Take Charge of Your Values

*Because They Guide
Your Decisions
and Shape Your Destiny*

This is what I believe: All decision making is really value clarification.

Chapter 15

Be Led by Your Values, Not Just by Your Feelings

For many years, I didn't know whether to stay single forever or get married.

I joined a celibate brotherhood, visited three monasteries and interviewed dozens of priests. I even talked to Bishop Ted Bacani and told him, "Bishop, I've always been an organizer all my life. If I do become a priest, can I found my own congregation?"

I was half expecting he'd laugh uproariously and drive me out of his house.

But he took me seriously and said, "Let's continue to talk about it."

But there were also times when I longed and pined for marriage.

OK, that's tweaking the truth.

More honestly, I longed and pined for a beautiful woman beside me.

The thought of whispering sweet nothings to her under the moonlight, holding her hand, seeing her smile at me, spending our lives together…

I was a hopeless romantic.

But that's what I couldn't figure about myself.

What's a man to do?

Whether I were to get married or become a priest, I wanted to love God.

This was the ultimate purpose of my life.

The question was this: How could I best love God?

It would have been easy to be led by my feelings. At any given moment, I was emotionally pulled in one of these two directions.

But I realized it wouldn't work.

I had to be led by something far deeper than just my emotions.

Asking "Why" Exposes Your Values

As part of my discernment, I had to ask myself these two questions:

1. Why do I want to be celibate?

2. Why do I want to get married?

After years of searching through the confusion of my heart, I was finally able to answer these two questions — thus defining the *values* that were important to me.

1. I wanted to be celibate because I valued freedom.
2. I wanted to be married because I valued intimacy.

Let me define to you what *freedom* meant to me.

I loved the idea that, as a celibate, I could sail off to a tiny island anytime and take a one-week retreat. Anytime, I could pull out my wallet and give all my money away to a beggar on the street. Anytime, I could give all my belongings to the poor.

But *intimacy* pulled my heart strongly, too.

The idea that I could have a life partner.

The idea that I could serenade her, and that she would blow kisses to me, and that I could tell her that I loved her more than the world.

Putting these two values in front of me forced me to ask the question, "Which is more important to me? Freedom or intimacy?"

Decision Making Becomes Easier

This is what I believe: *All decision making is really values clarification.*

Anytime I'm having a hard time making a decision, it simply means that I'm *not* clear with my values.

When I was 30 years old, I knew I had to make a decision for my future.

I went up a mountain and had a personal retreat guided by a wise Jesuit.

In that retreat, I felt God speak to my heart, *"My will for your life is your deepest desire."*

These words shocked me.

It rocked my world.

I realized that if He made every fiber of my being, He designed me.

I just needed to follow my design!

So I had to ask myself the question, *What is more important to me? Freedom or intimacy?*

At the end of my mountain retreat, I had my answer.

It was a difficult choice, but I had to choose which value was more important to me.

Two years later, I met Bishop Ted Bacani again.

He agreed to officiate my wedding.

Chapter 16

Values Are Your Internal Compass

When you're lost in a jungle, you need a compass.

Because the compass — no matter how you shake it, twirl it, spin it or flip it — will always point north.

The Seven Habits of Highly Effective People author Stephen Covey says our values are like the internal compass of our soul.

If you don't know where to go, all you have to do is to look at your internal compass — your values in life.

Here's the truth: *In the end, long-term happiness can only come from consistently living by our highest values.*

A Choice Between Ease or Peace

I write with passion.

When I write, I'm so focused, I get lost in a different world.

That's why when my tiny son enters my home office and asks, "Daddy, can you play with me?" I get agitated. It's like I'm driving a race car at 200 kilometers per hour and someone spikes my tires to shreds — and I hear the deafening sound of metal on gravel.

So I take a deep breath and ask myself a quick question: "What is my highest value? *Efficiency or love?*"

And as if it was hit by a 10-foot wave, my irritation is swept away.

I look at my happy son with expectant eyes and say, "What do you want to play, son?" He takes my hand and leads me to his room. We sit on the floor and build castles, bridges and towers with wooden blocks — all the time talking, laughing and singing.

I have the greatest time in my life.

And I almost missed it.

Your Values Are Built on God's Laws

What is the "north" of your internal compass?

To the north is God's Laws. And north will *never* change.

"Heaven and earth will pass away, but my words shall not pass away."[1]

---

[1] *Matthew 24:35 (NIV)*

I remember one story about President Ramon Magsaysay, which I think is more legend than fact, but I'll share it anyway.

One day, Magsaysay was complaining about why sugar prices were down. His economist told him, "Well, sir, we can't do anything about it. It's the law of supply and demand." Magsaysay got angry and said, "Who made that law? I'm the President of the Republic! *Repeal that law!*"

An awkward silence hung in the air. People looked at each other, wondering who would be the courageous one to correct the President. Finally, one guy had the courage to say, "Sir, the law of supply and demand is like the law of gravity. We cannot repeal that, sir."

At that, the President banged his fist on the table and said, "I'm the President! I will repeal the law of gravity!"

The Law of Love, the Law of Forgiveness, the Law of Justice, the Law of Holiness, the Law of Purity... These are absolute laws! They cannot be repealed. If we don't follow them, we destroy ourselves.

These laws are written in our hearts, and they become our values.

"Indeed, when the Gentiles, who do not have the law, do by nature things required by the law, they are a law for themselves, since they show that the requirements of the law are written on their hearts."[2]

Didn't you notice? The essence of the Ten Commandments is found in all ancient cultures. Murder is always wrong. Honoring your parents is always right. Stealing is always wrong. Love is always beautiful.

Why?

Because God made us, built us, designed us with this internal compass.

We were made for love, honesty, forgiveness, freedom and faithfulness.

Our job is to always follow our internal compass. If we follow our internal compass, then we will always have a sense of peace, a sense of certainty, a total congruency that few people experience.

---

[2] *Romans 2:14 (NIV)*

Make a List

Many years ago, I asked myself what my Top 10 values were. I came up with a powerful list: love, courage, honesty, humility, faithfulness, simplicity, generosity, endurance, wisdom and health.

I resolved that whenever I made a decision, I would consult this list.

So far, making choices based on this list has been wonderful! I've saved myself from a lot of regret, even if the decision turned out to be a mistake. Why? Because I made the decision from a pure conscience.

So here's my final advice: *List down your values.*

Ask yourself what is most important to you — and write them down!

Then consult the list whenever you make any decision in life.

Remember: Your values shape your destiny.

Live well!

Action Steps

Take Charge of Your Values

1. Look back at the major decisions you've made in the past. Were you guided by your values or by other factors — such as your feelings, what other people will say, or external circumstances?

2. What are your highest values? What is most important to you? Write them on a card and stick it in your diary or Bible, in a place where you can see this list daily.

Take Charge of Your Time

*Give Your 10,000 Hours
and You Will Succeed*

If you want big returns, big success, big rewards in your life, you have to give 10,000 hours into what you love to do.

Chapter 17

Give 10,000 Hours

You can succeed in life.

Anybody can.

Because time is the great equalizer.

Every human being is given the same amount of time. A billionaire in New York has 24 hours. A beggar in Quiapo has 24 hours. It's really what we do with those 24 hours that impacts our lives.

Malcolm Gladwell wrote about the 10,000-Hour Rule in his book, *Outliers.* He believed that greatness requires the giving of enormous time — approximately 10,000 hours — to what you do.

The Phenomenon from London — or from Germany?

One of his examples was The Beatles.

The Beatles is the most successful band in the history of music. You must forgive me as I will only tell you what I heard from others. Growing up, I actually never heard The Beatles. I'm only familiar with Charice Pempengco and Sarah Geronimo. (Wink.)

Some say The Beatles were very successful because they were simply super talented.

That's not completely true.

Talent isn't enough.

Talent is overrated.

Do you know of very talented people who are unsuccessful?

I do. I also know there are millions of them around.

According to Gladwell, The Beatles were successful because of what happened in Hamburg, Germany from 1960 to 1964.

What was so special about Hamburg, Germany?

It wasn't that they paid well. (They didn't.) Or that they had the best equipment. Or that they had the best music scene.

Hamburg was special because of the huge amount of time you were forced to spend performing every single day.

In Hamburg, if your band was hired by a club, they'd make you perform from Monday to Saturday, eight hours a day, nonstop.

Do the math. If The Beatles performed over 1,200 times, multiply each performance by eight hours. That's

10,000 hours of playing time in a span of four years.

So by the time they returned to England, The Beatles "sounded like no one else." And the rest was history.

I repeat: Give your 10,000 hours in one area, and you unlock your greatness in that area.

Why He Became the Richest Man in the World

Bill Gates is another example Gladwell gave of the 10,000-Hour Rule.

How did he become the richest man in the world?

Was it because he was a super genius?

Or was it something else that happened when he was a kid?

In 1968, Bill Gates was only 13 years old when he attended a private high school. It was one of the very few high schools on Planet Earth that had a computer.

Bill Gates was only 13 years old when he fell in love with the computer. He was totally fascinated by it. He couldn't do anything else except write computer programs.

When everyone was asleep, he would sneak out of his house at midnight, run to the school, slip into the computer room, and use the computer until the wee hours of the morning. He'd go back home before dawn to get ready to go back to school.

Remember what I told you — that successful people are a little bit crazy? That's Bill Gates.

By the time he hit 18 years old, he had already logged in 10,000 hours of computer programming — at a time when very few people in the world even knew what a computer was.

Let me give you some of *my* examples.

Teen Idol Becomes a Servant

My friend, Adrian Panganiban, is a fantastic singer.

One reason: he started singing on TV at the age of four.

A few years later, he became a teen idol.

He was part of The Big 4, together with Lala Aunor, Winnie Santos and Boyet Orca.

Adrian told me that during that time, he would have concerts every day — flying from one town to another, sometimes from one country to another. Sometimes he would have to sleep on the bus or plane, performing back-to-back concerts.

Adrian had put in his 10,000 hours of performing before huge crowds, unlocking his greatness in that area.

But today, he's giving that greatness to God.

Today, Adrian still performs in concerts.

But he sees himself more as a servant than a star.

Let me introduce you to another friend.

Theater Actor Becomes a Preacher

I see myself in George Gabriel.

I'm not just talking about our great looks. (Didn't I say that successful people are a little bit crazy?)

I'm talking about the fact that George gave his life to God when he was 12 years old — the exact age I gave my life to God.

George was willing to do anything for God. He sang, he led worship, he did concerts, he preached, he played the drums, and he became a theater actor.

When he had a musical, he performed on stage every day, twice a day, Monday to Friday.

Very easily, George clocked in 10,000 hours of performance.

Today, this theater actor doesn't do musicals anymore.

But he continues to preach with his powerful theatrical skills.

George is now 36 years old.

That means that for the past 24 years, he's been serving God.

That's much more than 10,000 hours, believe me.

What's my message?

If you want big returns, big success, big rewards in your life, you have to give 10,000 hours to what you love to do.

Chapter 18

Give 10,000 Hours to Your Family

The 10,000-Hour Rule of Greatness works in any area.

Question: Do you want to be great in your family life?

Many marriages are failing because of neglect.

Give 10,000 hours to your marriage — and it will prosper.

Why is it that before the wedding, boyfriends and girlfriends spend so much time together? They love talking to each other, laughing their hearts out and hanging out together.

But the moment the wedding happens, they forget all that.

If you want your marriage to work, work on your relationship. Spend time with each other. Go out on dates each week, more if necessary.

And do you want to be great parents?

Quality Time Isn't Enough

I've spent many hours talking with parents whose kids are drifting away from God and hanging out with the wrong crowd.

I know my next statement is very simplistic.

But bear with me.

I believe kids get into trouble *usually* because their parents didn't spend enough time with them. Parents failed to unlock the greatness of their children by not spending both quantity and quality time with them.

All is not lost.

Reach out to them now.

Tell them you love them. Go out of your way and spend time with them.

The other night, I went home totally exhausted. I told my family I was going to sleep early.

But after I dozed off on bed, my then five-year-old son entered the room and wanted to jump on a trampoline.

In his mind, my body was a giant trampoline!

He'd step on me, walk on me and jump on me.

A part of me wanted to say, "Francis, not now. Daddy is really tired."

But the words couldn't leave my lips.

Because I knew that a time will come when he'll no longer play with me that way. A day will come when he's all grown up and he won't jump on me anymore. (At least, I hope he won't!) While we can play together, I'll do it.

I've said no to my kids when they ask for toys.

I've said no to my kids when they ask for junk food.

I've said no to my kids when they ask for gadgets.

But to this day, I've never said no when they ask for my *time*. No matter how busy or how tired I am.

I urge you: Give 10,000 hours to your kids and you will unlock their greatness.

When you spend your time loving, you're doing something that will last forever. When you love, you're planting a tree in the soil of heaven.

Chapter 19

Give 10,000 Hours to God

Here's my final message: Give 10,000 hours to your relationship with God.

Put God first. Prioritize Him. Seek Him first.

I don't want to complicate things, so let me just put three things before you.

Here's the number one thing: Give at least 10 minutes a day to connect with God.

I recommend reading the Bible every day.

To know what to read, I suggest you use a Bible guide — such as *Didache, Companion* and *Sabbath*. I heard that those who write and publish those Bible guides are really fantastic people. (He, he.)

Even if you don't understand what the Bible is saying, just keep reading. Clock in your 10,000 hours.

In due time, you'll understand.

If you want to receive Bible reflections in your inbox every day, join my international, non-physical, borderless, virtual community called *Kerygma Family.* Log on to www.KerygmaFamily.com now!

Here's my second recommendation: Join a prayer meeting every week to nourish your soul. If you don't have one, I invite you to The Feast. We have dubbed it "the happiest place on earth." For more information on schedules and venues, visit www.LightFam.com.

Make it a non-negotiable item in your schedule.

Don't miss feeding your spirit.

And here's number three: Give your time to God by serving Him in the people around you.

"I Wasted 60 Years"

Many years ago, when I was still a teenager, a woman called me up to pray for her sick husband. "Ben is 61 and he's dying," she said, her voice breaking. "My husband has cancer."

That happened a long time ago, but I can never forget Ben. Meeting him had such an incredible impact on my life.

The next day was Valentine's Day. I was single and had no date, so I told her, "I'll visit your husband tomorrow and he'll be my Valentine's date."

The next morning, I saw their huge home. The woman told me that her husband was a doctor — a very successful one.

When I entered the living room, I saw him seated on a chair, wearing his pajamas.

I tried to imagine him before his sickness.

A strong man. A powerful doctor. So in control of life.

Now, he was a broken man. Totally dependent on others.

We greeted each other.

"Hi, Dr. Ben," I said, "before I pray over you, can you tell me your story?"

He nodded. "My doctors discovered the cancer in my body. They gave me six months to live. That was eight months ago. I'm living on extra time."

"Wow..."

"Bo, when I found out I had cancer, I prayed to God. I started going to Mass on Sundays. I even went to a prayer meeting with my wife. I was too busy to do all those things before. Bo, I wasted 60 years of my life!"

That was when he began to cry.

Here was a successful man, sobbing before me.

In between sobs, he said, "But... but... after a while, I had to stay home because of the pain in my body. Most days, I cannot do anything else but lie down in bed..."

He gripped my hand.

"Bo, please..." he said, "I want you to pray that

God extend my life. Even a little bit more. Just a little bit more. Because all these years, I was very busy earning money. I didn't spend time with God. I want to serve Him… I have so many plans. So many things I want to do for Him. If only He'll give me more time."

I prayed over him.

Driving home, I felt God was speaking to me through this man's life.

When I arrived home, I knelt down and said, "Lord, when I grow old, I don't want to be like Dr. Ben. I don't want to have regrets in my life. While I'm young, I want to serve You."

You Hang on to Life by a Mere Thread;
It Can Snap Anytime

I read somewhere that three people die every second.

Tick. Tick. Tick. Tick. Tick…

That's 15 people who died in the past five seconds.

If it took you 15 minutes to read this chapter, 2,700 people would have already died in the world. (When you're done reading, please check your pulse. Just in case you were part of the 2,700…)

Friend, life is so incredibly fragile.

You hang on to life by a mere thread.

Anytime, it can snap.

Every moment is a great gift from God.

The Bible says, "Teach us how short our life is, so that we may become wise."[1] You see, God never promised that you'll wake up tomorrow morning. Every time you wake up in the morning, you should throw a party. Celebrate! It's an undeserved gift.

While You Have Breath

While you're alive, I urge you to give your time to God.

While you have breath, love God.

While you're still strong, love the people in your life.

Jesus says, "As long as it is day, we must keep on doing the work of him who sent me; night is coming when no one can work. While I am in the world, I am the light of the world."[2] Jesus knew that night was coming "when no one can work."

All of us will one day face that "night."

Today, I want to remind you of that stark reality.

---

[1] *Psalms 90:12, GNB*
[2] *John 9:4-5, NIV*

Here's a suggestion. To know how short your life is, count the number of Sundays you have left.

I read that the average life expectancy in the Philippines is 66 years old. That's pretty short.

There are 3,432 Sundays in 66 years.

I'm now 44. That means I've already used up 2,288 Sundays.

If I live until 66, I only have 1,144 Sundays to go.

One thousand one hundred forty-four Sundays only!

My gosh.

I read this somewhere.

If you want to be reminded about how short your life is, I suggest you get a jar of seeds.

Any kind of seed would do.

The seeds should be the exact number of Sundays you have left in your life (based on the average life expectancy).

Then every Sunday, remove one seed from the jar.

Every week, you'll see the seeds in the jar decrease.

When you reach 66 years old, and no seeds are left, each Sunday becomes a big bonus from God.

Use Your Time Well Because You Can't Replace It

You can replace lost things. Money. Cell phones. Cars. Houses. But you can't replace lost time.

Remember the jar with the seeds inside?

Each moment of your life is a seed.

When you remove a seed from the jar, you have a choice.

It's the choice you are given at every single moment.

You can throw the seed away and lose it forever.

Or you can plant it in soil and make it eternal.

What am I saying?

When you spend your time loving, you're doing something that will last forever.

When you love, you're planting a tree in the soil of heaven.

According to Dr. Ben, he threw away his seeds for the first 60 years of his life. He wasted them. He spent them in selfishness.

Don't make that mistake.

I invite you to give each moment to God.

Spend your life loving people.

Heaven is waiting for your seeds.

Action Steps

Take Charge of Your Time

1. Do the Jar Project. Compute the number of Sundays you have left and fill a jar with seeds or beans equal to that number. Then resolve to make every seed count.

2. Make your bucket list — the things you want to do in your lifetime. Take the top five and start doing something each day to achieve those things. Don't wait to get married, to get a job promotion or to retire before doing those things.

3. Who are the people in your life that you need to spend more time with? Schedule regular dates with them. Do it now.

Take Charge of Your Talent

*The World Is Waiting
for Your Gift*

Be who God created you to be. Be yourself. And you'll succeed.

Chapter 20

3 Powerful Steps to Give Your Talent

Some years back, I asked my then five-year-old Francis to sing on stage. Right after his song, I asked my then 10-year-old son Bene to preach.

This was before thousands of people at The Feast, our weekly prayer gathering.

It was awesome.

Francis brought the house down with his cute singing.

And Bene blew the audience away with his talk.

Hey, please understand.

I'm the father.

So my report is highly biased.

Because I'm sure my kids made mistakes on stage.

Francis probably sang off-key a couple of times.

He probably sang out of rhythm during some parts of his song.

And Bene probably committed grammatical errors.

He might have mispronounced words.

But all that didn't matter.

I didn't pay too much attention to their mistakes.

Because the whole time they were on stage, my heart was bursting within me, saying over and over again, "Those are my kids!"

This doesn't *just* happen when they're performing in front of a crowd of people. I get the same feeling when I watch my kids draw, swim, play, talk…

In other words, I just love it when they're themselves.

People ask me, "Bo, when Bene grows up, he'll be a preacher like you. He's such a good speaker."

I answer them, "I don't know. That's up to him to decide."

I've always told Bene, "Be who God created you to be. Be yourself. And you'll succeed."

God Loves It When You Become You

Friend, God is a father, too.

When you use your talent, God's heart is bursting with pride.

When He sees you performing on the stage of life, using the talent that He has given you to bless the world, God is saying, "That's MY kid!"

Why? *God loves it when you become you.*

He wired you to do something.

He designed you, formed you, shaped you, rigged you, tooled you and wired you to be a special gift to the world.

If He designed you to be an anthropologist, be an anthropologist.

If He designed you to make deals, then make deals.

If He designed you to listen, then listen.

If He designed you to count money, then count money.

If He designed you to plant crops, then plant crops.

If He designed you to fix cars, then fix cars.

If He designed you to hold a camera, then hold a camera.

I repeat: *God loves it when you become you.*

Three Landmarks in Your Success Journey

Friend, do you want to be successful in life?

Remember that success doesn't happen overnight.

Success is a journey.

In fact, you'll have to pass by three landmarks on this journey. Between where you are now and where your success is are three landmarks. Here they are:

Landmark 1: When you discover your talent.

Landmark 2: When you develop your talent.

Landmark 3: When you deliver your talent.

These three landmarks correspond to the three kinds of people in the world.

There are people who haven't discovered their talents because they've dug a hole in the ground — the hole of low self-worth — and hid their talent there.

They feel useless.

They feel they're condemned to live a mediocre life.

I should know.

I was once such a person…

Chapter 21

Step 1: Discover Your Talent

All of us possess various talents.

Some can dance like Gary V.

Some can make people laugh like Michael V.

Some can act like *Ate* Vi.

While some can make burgers like Jollivee.

(Sorry for the corny joke, I slept late last night.)

But I didn't believe this years ago.

When I was a kid, I used to complain to God, "Lord, why didn't You give me any talents?" I felt as if I was the most talentless person on the planet.

I was afflicted with *comparisonitis*.

When I was in Grade 5, I had a classmate in school who seemed to have all the talents I wanted to have.

His name was Ariel.

He was number one in class.

He was number one in basketball.

He was number one in baseball.

He was number one among the girls.

He was number one among the teachers.

Me?

I was number one at being nothing.

I was number one at being unpopular.

I was number one at being bullied by the bullies.

I was number one at being the laughingstock of my teachers.

But I had one talent that I thought I was good at. At least I had one. I knew I was good at drawing.

But one day, we had art class. And Ariel drew something that was Walt Disney material. He was number one again.

I complained to God. I said, "Lord, how unfair! Why is he number one in drawing, too? That was my only talent."

But one fateful day, everything changed in my life. That was the day I discovered my talent.

All You Have to Do Is Say Yes

As a 13-year-old kid, I was attending this small prayer meeting with my parents. And in one of those meetings, our leader announced to everyone, "God spoke to me last night. One of you will preach the Gospel all over the world."

She then approached me and asked, "Bo, can you give a talk next Friday?"

Imagine. Me. That skinny, pip-squeaky kid, who read *Superman* comics and watched *Voltes V* on TV, was asked to give a talk.

And with my pre-puberty, high-pitched voice, I said, "Sure!"

That was the only thing that God was asking from me.

To say yes to His call.

Did I know I could give a talk?

No.

But I was willing to try.

I could have given in to fear — and said no.

If I did, I wouldn't be preaching at The Feast every Sunday today.

Imagine if I hadn't said yes. What would I be doing now?

The thought gives me the shivers.

But on that day, I conquered my fear and said yes.

When I gave my talk, I realized I had the gift of peace.

Because when I spoke, I was more powerful than Valium. Because I made everyone fall asleep.

I remember this one woman sitting in the front row.

She slept so soundly during my talk, her mouth was wide open. So open, I could count how many of her molars were filled.

I felt humiliated. I was such a poor speaker!

After my talk, I sat down and told myself, "I'll never give another talk in my entire life."

Your Availability Is More Important than Your Ability

But my prayer group leader, bless her, approached me again and asked me, "Bo, why don't you give another talk next week?"

And I looked at her with the steely gaze of a hurt, humiliated, 13-year-old kid, and said, "Sure!"

I kept saying yes to God.

And this is what I've found out: *When you give to God your availability, He will supply you with your ability.*

I discovered my gift.

After a few months, I became a better speaker.

And the woman in the front row who slept during my talk?

She kept on sleeping during all my talks.

I realized she was an insomniac. And that the only time she could sleep was when someone was speaking.

Why You Haven't Discovered Your Talents

A lot of people ask me that question: How will I discover my talent? Kids ask me that question a lot. Teens ask me that question a lot. Amazingly, even adults ask me that question a lot.

Let me be frank with you.

One of the biggest reasons why you haven't discovered your talent is because you haven't been saying yes to life. You've been habitually saying no.

To opportunities. To learning. To experiences. To stretching.

You've been saying no because you're afraid.

You're afraid of making mistakes.

You're afraid of being laughed at by people.

You're afraid of falling flat on your face.

You're afraid of being humiliated.

Discovering your talent is like discovering buried treasure.

Treasure hunters don't dig in one spot and automatically find the treasure. Treasure hunters survey the area thoroughly.

They dig in one spot, find nothing, dig in another spot again, find nothing again, dig in another spot again, find nothing again… until they dig in this one spot and find the treasure!

God has called you to serve Him with your talent.

So serve Him and be willing to make mistakes.

Be willing to fail.

Be willing to be a fool for Christ.

All you have to do is say yes to God!

Chapter 22

Step 2: Develop Your Talent

I didn't stop at discovering my talent.

I developed it.

Some people discover their talent, but they don't develop it.

They're good mechanics, farmers, speakers, writers, thinkers, listeners, musicians, engineers, mathematicians, administrators — but they don't develop their talent.

They don't hone their craft.

They don't sharpen their saw.

They don't expand their expertise.

They don't increase their initiatives.

They don't grow their gift.

How did I develop my talent?

Simple.

I used it.

I said yes to every single invitation given to me to speak.

Tiny prayer groups invited me to speak; I said yes.

Prisons invited me to speak; I said yes.

Hospitals invited me to speak; I said yes.

Poor dilapidated schools in far-flung barrios invited me to speak; I said yes.

I had to cross three rivers before I could speak; I said yes.

Only 20 people showed up; I said yes.

Only 10 people showed up; I said yes.

Only three people showed up; I said yes.

In my early years, I would preach every single day.

I didn't know it then, but saying yes to every invitation was fulfilling Malcolm Gladwell's 10,000-Hour Rule of Greatness.

Sometimes, young preachers come up to me and tell me, "Brother Bo, I want to preach as well as you do."

"Great!" I say. So I ask them, "How often do you preach?"

"Oh, about once a month…" they say.

I want to strangle them. "Once a month? By the time you'll be any good, you'll be 150 years old. You should be preaching every single day! Create opportunities for you to speak!"

Here's the truth: The only way to develop your talent is to use it.

Let me say it again. If you don't use it, you lose it.

One of the things I've found out about this world is that you don't get rewarded for discovering your talent. You don't get rewarded for developing your talent. You only get rewarded for delivering your talent.

Chapter 23

Step 3: Deliver Your Talent

Some people discovered their talent, developed their talent, but don't *deliver their talent*.

For example, I have a friend who knows he's a good singer.

As a kid, he was already blessed with a fantastic voice.

He sings in his house every day to develop his voice.

But here's the funny thing: Not once has he volunteered to sing in public. Not in parties. Not in church. Not in programs. Not in weddings. One day, I invited him to join the music ministry and he said he had no time.

So far, the only ones who have heard him sing are his shower curtain, his bathroom mirror and his toilet bowl.

One of the things I've found out about this world is that you don't get rewarded for discovering your talent.

You don't get rewarded for developing your talent. You only get rewarded for delivering your talent.

In other words, do you have the ability to launch something?

Planning to launch it is not enough.

Preparing to launch it is not enough.

You have to actually launch it.

There are those who like tinkering with their work *endlessly.* So they delay. And delay. And delay. And they never launch.

It's the sickness of the corporate world.

Again, the reason why people don't deliver is fear.

It's the same old enemy.

They're afraid of failure.

They're afraid of rejection.

They're afraid of public humiliation.

So they want everything perfect before they launch.

And there lies the mistake.

There's no such thing.

They don't understand that perfection doesn't exist.

What you need to do is launch and relaunch and keep on relaunching until you get it right.

Here's what I realized: Before you become a public success, you first have to become a public humiliation!

It's the only way.

No One Is Exempt

Let me end with two stories.

A lot of people tell me, "Bo, I really have no talent."

I disagree.

Let me introduce you to a 21-year-old man named Jayjay.

Jayjay Ocaya sits on a wheelchair the whole day. Jayjay has kidney failure and goes for dialysis twice a week. Jayjay is also deaf.

He was born with a congenital disease called hydrocephalic spina bifida. That means his spinal column isn't fully developed. To survive, he has to go through dialysis twice a week.

Yet every Sunday, Jayjay is part of our Warmth Ministry at The Feast in the Philippine International Convention Center (PICC). What is his talent? He may not be able to hear and he may not be able to walk, but he can smile.

Every Sunday, Jayjay smiles at people and shows them God's love.

Let me tell you about another friend. Her name is Ann Martha Padilla. She is a 26-year-old girl with cerebral palsy and she has to stay in bed the whole day.

She can't stand or walk or move the way she wants to. Her muscles move on their own. Her mother has to feed her, bathe her and carry her around.

She also can't talk the way you and I do.

If there's one person that has the right to say, "I have no talent," and, "I can't serve God," it would be Ann Martha Padilla.

But that's not true.

Because Ann Martha Padilla gave her yes to God.

And today, she has a powerful ministry.

She serves hundreds of people in a very personal way.

Ann Martha Padilla is an intercessor and an encourager.

The way she does it is through her cell phone.

She would grab her cell phone with her toes.

And with her other foot, she'd stab at the keypad. Every day, she'll send her prayers and inspiration to textmates all over the world.

She prays for her textmates every day.

She encourages them.

She inspires them.

She has discovered, developed and delivered her talent for God's people. And people are very blessed because of her.

Jayjay and Ann Martha have found their talent, now it's your turn.

Give your talent to God.

Just say yes to Him.

Action Steps

Take Charge of Your Talent

1. Make an inventory of the things you can do. Don't limit yourself to talents and skills like singing and writing or administration and leadership. Include things like friendliness toward strangers, patience with difficult people, even listening and giving advice to others.

2. Among the things in your list, mark those you need to develop, and those you've developed somehow but need to deliver to the world. What steps do you need to take to develop the talents you've already discovered? Where can you deliver the talents you've already developed?

Take Charge of Your Treasure

How to Use Your Pain to Achieve Great Success

All permanent success comes from pain. Any success that doesn't come from pain will be short-lived.

Chapter 24

Two Gigantic Gifts of Giving

When we give, we receive two gifts.

The first gift of giving is prosperity.

I hope you know that by now. The Bible says that when you give, you receive "pressed down, shaken together, and running over."[1] (We like hearing it more in Tagalog: *siksik, liglig at umaapaw*.)

Everybody talks about this first gift.

But very few people talk about the second gift of giving — *pain*.

When you give, you experience pain.

No one likes pain.

I know I don't.

We avoid it at all costs.

That's why many people avoid diets, doctors and dentists.

---

[1] *Luke 6:38*

But let me give you a startling fact…

We *need* pain to survive.

We need pain to succeed in life.

In fact, *all permanent success comes from pain.*

Any success that doesn't come from pain will be short-lived.

Check out these lotto winners.

In March 2012, Dionie Reyes shared how he won P14 million through the lotto — and spent it all in three months — through gambling, womanizing and drinking. Now, he's not only bankrupt, he also owes someone P500,000.

In the US, it's even worse. Michael, a garbage collector, won $15 million from the lotto (or lottery, as they call it over there). But after just a few years, he lost all his money and is now trying to get his old job back as a garbage collector.

There's another guy named Jack who won a staggering $315 million from the lotto. But he, too, lost everything after less than 10 years. But he didn't only lose the money — he also lost his family.

They're not alone. Go ahead, Google "lotto winners lose money" and you'll get hundreds of true-to-life tragic stories.

In fact, many lotto winners say it was a nightmare and wished they had never won. Because of their winning, their marriages broke up, their families disintegrated, their children turned to drugs, and they lost all their happiness. Easy come, easy go.

I repeat: Real success comes from pain.

If it didn't come from pain, it isn't real success.

Hypothermia

Let me talk about hypothermia.

Hypothermia is a physical condition whereby your body's core temperature drops below 35 degrees Celsius and all body functions, shut down, including your ability to feel pain.

Remember the movie *Titanic?*

Our hero, Jack, died of hypothermia.

And many people who escaped the Titanic before it sank eventually died of hypothermia in the freezing waters of the Atlantic Ocean. Because they could no longer feel pain, they just fell asleep and drowned.

Mountain climbers conquering Mt. Everest who get trapped in sub-zero temperature try hard to wake themselves up. They intentionally let themselves feel pain to survive.

What does this have to do with you?

Let me explain.

Do You Suffer from Non-Physical Hypothermia?

I know of people who have non-physical hypothermia.

They've become so comfortable in life.

They've become soft. They've become lax. They've become sleepy. And their life has become meaningless. They no longer have burning dreams in their lives. And they've started to die a slow death.

Why?

Because there's no pain.

I now realize that pain is essential to grow in any area of your life — spiritually, relationally or financially.

How do you wake up from hypothermia? Pain.

Chapter 25

First Source of Pain: Grief

There are three sources of inner pain…
The first pain comes from *Grief.*
The second pain comes from *Greed.*
And the third pain comes from *Giving.*
Let me discuss grief first.

My Guess: 90 Percent of Successful People Went Through Intense Pain

I can't prove this with scientific research.

But from the past 30 plus years of meeting first-generation, financially successful people, 90 percent of them went through intense pain before they achieved success. And they were able to use that inner pain to fuel their rise to the top.

Let me share with you the stories of four very successful people and how they used their pain to become successful in life.

Zig Ziglar

Zig Ziglar is a bestselling author and one of the most well-loved motivational speakers in the world.

Yet he grew up in poverty. Zig was the tenth of 12 children. And to make things worse, his father died when he was only six years old.

And life was very hard.

As a small child, he had to work. He worked in a grocery store from 4:30 a.m. to 11:00 p.m. every day. In case you can't do the math, that's an 18-hour workday — and for a kid at that!

Fast forward a few years later. Poverty still followed him.

When Zig got married, he applied for work as a salesman.

But for the first two years, he couldn't sell his products.

So he had to sell his furniture just so he and his wife could eat. When his daughter was born, the hospital bill was $64. He didn't even have $64 — and had to go out and sell something so he could take his family home.

It was these hardships that fueled his desire to succeed in life.

And succeed, he did. In one year, he became the number one salesman of his company. And later on, he set up his own company and became very successful in life.

Mary Kay Ash

When her marriage failed, Mary Kay became a single mother with three kids. She could hardly make ends meet.

At the time, she was working as a saleswoman for Stanley Home Products, but she wasn't doing too well in her job. When the company had an annual sales conference, she wanted so badly to go. But she had no money.

So she borrowed money to go there. She also brought with her a bag of biscuits. That was what she ate for the three days of the conference.

But in that conference, she saw a salesperson go up on stage to receive the Number One Salesperson of the Year Award. When she saw that, she went up to Mr. Stanley, the owner of the company, and told him that she'd be the next person who would win that award. He smiled and said, "I believe you will."

The following year, she did go up on stage to receive the Number One Salesperson of the Year award.

Later on, she built her own company, Mary Kay Cosmetics.

When she died in 2003, that single mother's company had 800,000 saleswomen and had already made $2 billion in annual sales.

Anthony Robbins

Tony Robbins grew up in a poor family.

He would steal food in grocery stores — just to be able to eat.

He couldn't even pay for his rented room.

His electricity was always about to be cut off.

And he couldn't answer the phone because he owed money to everyone he knew.

One of his most painful experiences was falling in love with a lady, but watching another suitor win her heart. The suitor picked her up in a very expensive car. Tony knew the girl loved him, but she also wanted to be comfortable. He knew he couldn't provide that for her, and he felt totally worthless.

All this pain became his driving force to get out of his hole.

Tony eventually started 15 companies and became a phenomenal success. This once-upon-a-time janitor has become an advisor to three US presidents, including President Clinton, and other heads of states, such as Mikhail Gorbachev, Margaret Thatcher, Francois Mitterrand and Nelson Mandela.

Joe Girard

Joe Girard had one business failure after another.

One day, he found himself without a job, without money, without savings. He experienced a whole year of poverty.

One morning, his wife told him, "Joe, we have no more food. And our kids are now out on the street begging."

That day, Joe left the house and applied for work as a car salesman.

He resolved in his heart that he had to sell a car that day so he could feed his hungry kids.

Before the day was over, he sold a car. He borrowed $10 from his manager. He rushed home with a brown bag of groceries. He was so happy that his family had food to eat that day.

All this pain became a burning fire in him to change his life.

In a few years, he became the *Guinness Book of World Records'* greatest car salesman in the world. The typical car salesman sold seven cars a month. Joe Girard sold six cars a day. That's 150 cars every single month.

Use Your Pain from Grief

Think about it: What is the biggest difference between successful and unsuccessful people?

It can't be talent. I know a lot of unsuccessful people who are more talented than successful people. It can't be academics. There are billionaires today who never finished high school.

No. I believe that the biggest difference between successful and unsuccessful people is their *response to pain.*

How do you respond to pain?

Pain is like fuel.

Combustible, flammable, ignitable fuel.

But like real fuel, pain can do two things.

Fuel can explode or energize. It can explode and destroy everything around it. Or it can energize a rocket to the moon.

What am I saying?

Pain can *destroy* you or *develop* you.

It depends on how you respond to your pain.

If you respond with faith, pain can be the inner driving force that can change your life. Pain can be your fuel to rocket your launch to success.

Right now, you may be experiencing a lot of pain.

Perhaps your family life is a mess.

Perhaps your job situation is very tough.

Perhaps you always have no money.

Friend, this is not the end of your story.

You can overcome.

You can rise above your problems.

You can use your pain and let it fuel you to succeed in life. You can rocket your way out of your pain and into prosperity.

But just as a warning, let me talk about the second source of pain…

A greedy person is so obsessed with money, he doesn't stop working even if his way of working is killing him.

Chapter 26

Second Source of Pain: Greed

Greed is painful.

Greed will not let you sleep, rest or become complacent.

Some people become rich because of greed.

Perhaps they started with grief. Perhaps they grew up poor and had so much pain making ends meet — and this started their journey to wealth.

But after a while, greed took over.

No matter how much money they have, they want more and more and more. They're never satisfied. Their greed keeps manufacturing pain. They want bigger homes and bigger cars and bigger yachts and bigger diamonds.

But this kind of inner pain is deadly. It's the pain that will ultimately kill. Because greed leads to empty success.

I compare greed to gluttony.

I know someone who is obese.

He weighs 340 pounds.

And yet every time I see him, he is eating.

Every time we meet, I see him holding a hamburger, a cheesecake, a *burrito* or a bag of chips.

I ask him, "Why are you still eating?"

While chewing, he says, "(Chomp) I can't (chomp) stop (chomp) eating."

"But it's killing you!"

"I (chomp) know (chomp)."

In the same way, a greedy person is so obsessed with money, he doesn't stop working even if his way of working is killing him.

Thankfully, there is another kind of inner pain.

A beautiful, liberating and transformational pain.

Chapter 27

Third Source of Pain: Giving

Giving is self-imposed pain.

Giving is voluntarily chosen.

By the way, when you give and you don't experience pain, you didn't really give. Your giving is fake.

When you give, it must hurt you.

When you give, it must shake you up.

When you give, it must disturb your existence.

When you give, it must wake you up from your complacency.

When you give, it must rock your world so much, it creates a hunger in you to keep on earning money so that you can keep on giving.

The Bible says, "I will not sacrifice to the Lord my God burnt offerings that cost me nothing."[1] That is why this pain heals.

---

[1] *2 Samuel 24:24*

This pain gives joy.

This pain blesses you.

It's a cheerful pain!

This pain comes when you give.

Why?

Success Must Have a Reason

Success must have a reason.

And I have found my reason for success!

I've asked this question many times: Why do I keep working, striving, dreaming, growing, expanding and increasing?

I have enough. Really.

My family and I have clothes on our back.

We have a roof over our heads.

We have food on our table three times a day.

We even have regular family vacations.

I repeat: We're OK.

Why do I keep working? Why do I keep expanding my businesses? Why do I try to earn more?

There's only one answer. So I can give more.

So I can love more.

So I can contribute more to God's work.

So I can give more to God's poor.

Oh, believe me, I'll never run out of dreams!

The dream of the Kingdom is like a burning bush in my heart — unquenchable and eternal.

I pray that you find your reason for success.

I pray that you transform your pain — either from grief or giving — into fuel. Fuel to reach your dreams.

Action Steps

Take Charge of Your Treasure

1. Look back at the pain you have gone through in life. Were you able to harness it to bring you success today?

2. What pain are you going through today? Is it caused by grief, greed or giving?

3. Define your reason for success. What is the fuel that will drive you to reach your dreams?

Conclusion:

What Kind of Giver Are You?

There were three brothers named Jack, Ken and Poy.

One day, they were walking on the road. Each of them was carrying a *bayong* (native basket). They had just come from the field and harvested some potatoes.

Soon, they met an old poor man on the road, pulling a rickety cart behind him. He was dressed in rags and walking barefoot.

"What happened to you?" the brothers asked him.

The old man said, "My whole town has been flooded! Hundreds of people are now homeless, without food or water. They are very hungry. Can you give your sweet potatoes so I could feed my poor townspeople?"

Jack, Ken and Poy looked at each other and nodded their heads.

I'm telling you this story because Jack, Ken and Poy represent the three kinds of givers in the world today. I want you to find out what kind of giver you are.

Jack, the Token Giver

Jack reached down into his basket, pulled out three potatoes and placed them onto the cart of the old man.

The beggar said, "Thank you so much, my son."

Jack represents the first type of giver: The Token Giver.

All Jack does is give tokens of himself whenever he can.

In his family, he gives tokens of his time and energy to his kids and his wife — just enough so his wife won't leave him.

In his job, he does the barest minimum possible — so he won't get fired.

And in church, whenever the love offering basket is passed, he doesn't tithe — he gives tokens. Just to say that he gave.

Because of his habit of giving tokens, his returns are tiny.

He has a job but his career is stagnant.

His family lives in one house, but relationships are shallow.

He goes to church but hasn't grown spiritually.

Others however are like Ken...

Ken, the Tentative Giver

Ken did something different.

He brought his *bayong* near the cart, tilted it and poured out half of its contents.

The old beggar said, "Thank you very much, my son."

Ken represents the second type of giver in the world: The Tentative Giver.

He gives more than just tokens, but he still holds back.

In his family, he gives himself to them tentatively.

He has a 50/50 approach to relationships. Because of this, his relationships are average. Not great.

Let me tell you why.

I've been married for 14 years and here's one very important principle I've learned: Marriages don't work if the husband gives 50 percent and the wife gives 50 percent. *A marriage works only if both husband and wife give 100 percent to each other.*

When it comes to relationships, you don't measure what you give. You don't count. You throw away the ruler.

You don't say, "I rubbed your back; you should rub mine." That's not love; that's business. That's not love; that's a legal contract.

When you love a person, and you feel like you're giving more than he's giving you — don't be bitter. Because you know that even if you don't count, God is counting. And *the Law of the Universe will be the one to reward you.*

(Note: When I talk this way, I'm not talking about tolerating abusive, or drunkard, or philandering husbands. That's a totally different issue. I'm talking about healthy marriages here!)

In his job, it's the same: Ken gives satisfactory work. But not great work. He never goes beyond average. He never exceeds expectations.

How many of you know this? Promotions don't go to those with average performance. Promotions go to those with superior performance.

Ken hasn't been promoted. Because he doesn't take initiative or develops himself. He doesn't look for ways to become better, or get trained, or look for mentors.

In his spiritual life, it's the same story.

He tries to follow God but doesn't trust Him with his entire life. He holds back.

Not like Poy.

Poy, the Total Giver

It was Poy's turn.

Poy brought his *bayong* to the cart, inverted it and unloaded *everything*. He now carried an empty *bayong*.

The old man said, "Thank you very much, my son."

Poy represents the third kind of giver: The Total Giver.

Manny Pacquiao is a Poy in boxing.

Larry Bird is a Poy in basketball.

Gary V is a Poy in entertainment.

Jackie Chan is a Poy in making action movies.

Haven't you noticed? If you want to be successful, you have to be a little bit crazy. Insane. Illogical. Unreasonable. Fanatical.

Can you imagine doing 3,000 sit-ups every day?

Or making three-point shots with your eyes closed?

Or doing 2,900 retakes for one scene?

People who do such things are nuts.

But that's Poy.

Poy knows the magic of giving his all.

Note: You also realize that there are two types of successful people in the world. First are those who are successful in one field only — but are dismal failures in other areas. The second are those who are successful in the most important areas of their lives. And you find these people living among us. And that's what God wants for you!

Let me go back to Poy.

Poy gives his entire heart to his family. He doesn't want an OK marriage. He's committed to have a great marriage. He doesn't want to have an average relationship with his kids. Each day, he works to build deep bonds with them that will last forever.

In his job or business, Poy also works with passion. He loves what he does. And he loves his customers. For him, work is play. Because of this, he's proactive, takes initiative, gets training, hones his craft, and has a lifelong commitment to grow.

In his relationship with God, Poy completely surrenders himself to Him. He trusts God. He follows God all the way. He gives his time, his talent and his treasure to God.

I repeat my question: Which among these guys are you?

The Law of the Universe

My story isn't over.

As Poy stepped back with his empty *bayong*, lo and behold, the old beggar transformed and became a wizard!

Instead of tattered rags, he now wore a golden robe.

He had a long beard and his face was radiant.

The three brothers were so shocked, they could hardly speak or move.

The wizard said, "The Law of the Universe says that whatever you give, you shall receive. It's the Law of Reciprocity. So be ready to receive. How much will you receive? The measure that you used in giving will be the same measure used for rewarding you."

And in a flash — poof! — the wizard was gone.

The three brothers rubbed their eyes, wondering if it was all a dream. They walked home in a daze.

Because they were still in shock, none of them noticed that their *bayongs* were getting heavier with every step they took.

It was only when they reached home that they realized that something miraculous had happened.

All their *bayongs* were filled to the brim!

Jack opened his *bayong* and shouted, "Ken, Poy, look! The three potatoes that I gave the old man have been replaced with three bars of gold."

Ken opened his *bayong* and said, "Half of my *bayong* is now filled with gold bars!"

Poy opened his *bayong* and saw it filled with gold bars!

Once again, tell me, who are you? Jack, Ken or Poy?

Create a Bigger Vacuum

Once upon a time, I asked this question: Why is God so demanding?

Just look at the greatest commandment. Why does God want you to love Him with *all* your heart, with *all* your mind, and with *all* your strength (Matthew 22:37)?

Shouldn't He be satisfied if you love Him with half your heart, three-fourths of your mind, and 58 percent of your strength?

Why does God want you to give your all?

Helloooooow!

God doesn't need your time.

He's the owner of eternity. He invented time.

God definitely doesn't need your talents.

He can just snap His finger and 10,000 battalions of angels will kneel before Him to serve.

And obviously, God doesn't need your money.

He owns the universe.

So why does He want you to give your all?

Here's why:

When you give, *you create a vacuum.*

An empty space.

When I was a kid, my Grade 6 science teacher said, "Nature abhors a vacuum." Nature wants to automatically fill vacuums.

That's why vacuums are powerful magnets.

That vacuum — that empty space — attracts blessings. What blessings? The stuff that you gave away will be returned to you, only of far better quality and greater quantity.

Listen carefully. The more you give, the bigger the vacuum you create. The bigger the vacuum, the stronger the magnet — and the more blessings you'll attract into your life.

That's why giving your all is the secret of big returns.

There's magic when you give your *all.*

Because you also attract *all* that God wants to give to you.

This reminds me of a poor widow in the Bible.

The Secret of Big Returns

In Luke 21:1, it says…

Jesus saw the rich putting their gifts into the temple treasury. He also saw a poor widow put in two very small copper coins. "I tell you the truth," he said, "this poor widow has put in more than all the others. All these people gave their gifts out of their wealth; but she out of her poverty put in all she had to live on." (NIV)

How much are two small copper coins?

Scholars argue a lot here. These coins are called *lenta* in Greek. Many scholars believe that those two small copper coins are equal to around P25 in our currency today.

Here's something that you need to know: to be a poor old widow in biblical times was like experiencing hell on earth.

I'm serious. By law, she couldn't inherit the property of her husband. For this particular widow, her kids probably were very poor or didn't care for her — that's why she was poor.

Let me be honest with you.

If I were Jesus, and saw what she was about to do, I would have stopped her. I would have run to the widow and said, "Lady, please. Be practical. You don't have to give those two copper coins. How will you go home? Do you have something to eat tonight? Tomorrow? Hey, if you really want to give something, just give one. Because that's all you've got."

But Jesus didn't do that.

He did something very disturbing: He praised her.

He honored her to the high heavens. He put her on a pedestal for the entire world to imitate. He really thought she had done a great thing.

To Jesus, there's magic in "giving your all."

And that's what I want to share with you today.

Giving your all has incredible magic.

It's really the secret of big returns.

My Life

I've given my all to God.

Very imperfectly.

One of the things I gave to God was my youth. I started serving Him when I was 12 years old.

People ask me all the time, "Bo, don't you regret giving your life to God so early in life? You never 'tasted' the world."

I'd laugh.

And I'd tell them, "I've preached in 16 countries, visited 14 more nations, and preached in 38 cities in North America alone. I've written 30 bestselling books, lived in slum areas, built non-profit organizations, started 12 businesses, and talked to presidents, judges, and cardinals. The world has become my playground."

Because I gave my all to God, He has given it back to me a hundredfold.

Friend, I urge you: *Give your all to God.*

Nothing Is Too Small for God

And don't look down on how small your all is.

Nothing is too small for God.

Take a look at the Bible and see for yourself:

Moses used a simple walking stick to part the Red Sea and save an entire nation.

Gideon used a little trumpet to defeat the Midianite army.

Samson used a donkey's jawbone to slay a thousand Philistines.

David used a stone picked up from a river to knock down the giant Goliath — and win back the honor of Israel.

Elisha used a piece of cloth to divide the Jordan River.

Peter used his shadow to heal the sick in Jerusalem.

And Jesus used five pieces of bread to feed the multitudes.

All Is Never Small

Perhaps you feel that you're insignificant.

That you don't amount to anything.

You feel like you're that walking stick.

Or that little trumpet.

Or that jawbone.

Or that small stone.

Or that piece of cloth.

But I've got news for you: No matter how small you think you are, God has big plans for your life.

Really big plans!

I want you to believe that God has a big plan for your life.

Today, I urge you to take charge of your life and give your *all* to God, so that you can receive *all* the blessings He wants to give you.

May your dreams come true,

Bo Sanchez

P.S. *Get a unique, inspiring, powerful, personalized message from God each day.* Absolutely FREE! It'll blow you away. Sign up at **www.GodWhispersClub.com** now!

Free Resources for You:

1. Get a mountain load of spiritual nourishment for FREE at **www.KerygmaFamily.com** now! And join our borderless, international, non-physical community!

2. Download my FREE Ebook, *How to Know If Your Dreams Are God's Dreams,* at www.BoSanchez.ph now.

3. *Get a unique, inspiring, powerful, personalized message from God each day.* Absolutely FREE! It'll blow you away. Sign up at **www.GodWhispersClub. com** now!

About the Author

Bo Sanchez is a preacher, leader and entrepreneur. He is the author of 30 bestselling books and publisher of eight periodicals. Bo also has a weekly TV show, a daily radio program and a daily Internet TV show. He travels extensively around the world as a powerful speaker. So far, he has addressed audiences in 14 countries, including 36 cities in North America.

He founded many organizations, such as Anawim, a special home for the abandoned elderly, and Shepherd's Voice, a media group that publishes the widest read inspirational literature in the country. He is also the founder of the Light of Jesus Family, a spiritual community.

He was also cited as one of The Outstanding Young Men (TOYM) in 2006.

Privately, Bo is a successful entrepreneur. He frequently teaches and writes about financial literacy, believing that poverty is hugely a product of people's low financial I.Q., He focuses on subjects such as debt management, saving, investing and business.

In another endeavor he's very passionate about, Bo started the Catholic Filipino Academy (www. catholicfilipinoacademy.com) to help parents who want to homeschool their children.

But above all these, Bo believes that his first call is to be a loving husband to his wife, Marowe, and a devoted father to his sons, Benedict and Francis. They live in Manila, Philippines.

For more information, log on to his website www.bosanchez.ph or email him at bosanchez@ kerygmafamily.com.

By Joining the Kerygma Family, You Will Receive a Mountain Load of Blessings for Your Spiritual Life

Here's what will happen to you when you join the Kerygma Family:

1. You'll receive daily Bible reflections for your spiritual growth.

2. Each month, you'll get to read an online copy of *Kerygma,* the #1 Catholic inspirational magazine in the Philippines.

3. You'll belong to a borderless, global, non-physical community spread all over the world, connected through prayer and the desire for personal growth.

4. You shall have the special privilege of supporting this expansive work of the Lord (totally optional!), which includes Anawim, a ministry for the poorest of the poor, the abandoned elderly; Shepherd's Voice, a media ministry that uses TV, radio, print and the Internet to broadcast God's love to spiritually hungry people worldwide.

5. You and your intentions shall be included in our intercession team's prayers.

The KERYGMA Family

To join the KerygmaFamily, log on to www.kerygmafamily.com

Don't delay!

Start your day right.
Every day.

Subscribe now!